BROCK LESNAR

A&D Xtreme
BOLD HI-LO NONFICTION

An imprint of Abdo Publishing
abdobooks.com

ALEX MONNIG

ABDOBOOKS.COM

Published by Abdo Publishing, a division of ABDO, PO Box 398166, Minneapolis, Minnesota 55439. Copyright © 2024 by Abdo Consulting Group, Inc. International copyrights reserved in all countries. No part of this book may be reproduced in any form without written permission from the publisher. A&D Xtreme™ is a trademark and logo of Abdo Publishing.
Printed in the United States of America, North Mankato, MN.
052023
092023

THIS BOOK CONTAINS RECYCLED MATERIALS

Design: Kelly Doudna, Mighty Media, Inc.
Production: Mighty Media, Inc.
Editor: Katherine Chu
Cover Photograph: John Palmer/AP Images
Interior Photographs: Brian Wilkins/Flickr, p. 24; CelebrityArchaeology.com/Alamy Photo, pp. 28, 41; Don Feria/AP Images, pp. 16–17; Ed Webster/Flickr, pp. 34–35; JIM MONE/AP Images, pp. 30–31; John Locher/AP Images, pp. 1, 32–33; John Palmer/AP Images, pp. 8–9, 12–13, 14–15, 38–39; Jonathan Bachman/AP Images, pp. 18–19; Leonard Zhukovsky/Shutterstock Images, p. 22; Madison Square Garden Center/Wikimedia Commons, p. 8; MediaPunch Inc/Alamy Photo, pp. 20–21; Megan Elice Meadows/Flickr, pp. 4–5, 26–27; Miguel Discart/Flickr, pp. 36–37, 40; NCAA Photos/Getty Images, pp. 10–11; PHOTOlink/MediaPunch/AP Images, pp. 23, 25; REUTERS/Alamy Photo, pp. 42–43, 44; VCNW/iStockphoto, pp. 6–7; Wikimedia Commons, p. 29
Design Elements: amgun/Shutterstock Images (perspective); sanchesnet1/iStockphoto (spikes color, bolts); Wth/Shutterstock Images (stripes)

LIBRARY OF CONGRESS CONTROL NUMBER: 2022948814

PUBLISHER'S CATALOGING-IN-PUBLICATION DATA

Names: Monnig, Alex, author.
Title: Brock Lesnar / by Alex Monnig
Description: Minneapolis, Minnesota : Abdo Publishing, 2024 | Series: Xtreme wrestling royalty | Includes online resources and index.
Identifiers: ISBN 9781098291471 (lib. bdg.) | ISBN 9781098277932 (ebook)
Subjects: LCSH: Lesnar, Brock--Juvenile literature. | Wrestlers--Biography--Juvenile literature. | Actors--Biography--Juvenile literature. | World Wrestling Entertainment, Inc--Juvenile literature.
Classification: DDC 796.812092--dc23

TABLE OF CONTENTS

CHAPTER 1

ENDING THE STREAK

Brock Lesnar had one goal. It was to end Mark "the Undertaker" Calaway's series of 21 straight wrestling victories known as the **Streak**. In 2014, the two performed **amazing stunts** during WrestleMania XXX. Lesnar used three F5 wrestling moves. He then pinned the Undertaker, winning the match. Lesnar had ended the Streak!

Brock Lesnar uses his F5 move on Mark "the Undertaker" Calaway during WrestleMania XXX.

CHAPTER 2

FARM LIFE

Brock Edward Lesnar was born on July 12, 1977, in Webster, South Dakota. He grew up on his family's dairy farm. His family didn't have a lot of money and worked hard to make a living. They didn't even own a TV.

Brock entertained himself on the farm. At age five, he started wrestling. A few years later, he started lifting weights.

A farm in South Dakota. Brock played in the Lesnar family farm's hayloft. He would use it as a jungle gym and sometimes slept there as well.

When he was nine years old, Brock read magazines to learn more about weight training. He worked out at home and built his own **equipment** and weights with his father's help.

When in middle school, Brock found FLEX bodybuilding magazines at his school's library. He was also a big fan of famous bodybuilder Arnold Schwarzenegger.

CHAPTER 3

MAKING A NAME
ON THE MAT

Brock wrestled in high school and at Bismarck State College in North Dakota. In 1999, he had become good enough to be **recruited** by the University of Minnesota. He wrestled there until 2000.

While in college, Lesnar also started to watch World Wrestling Federation (WWF) shows. The WWF would become World Wrestling Entertainment (WWE) in 2002. WWE is a professional wrestling organization that features characters who perform in staged matches.

In 2000, Lesnar (*center*) won
the National Collegiate Athletic
Association heavyweight
national championship.

XTREME FACT

One of Lesnar's University of
Minnesota coaches was Shelton
Benjamin. He also became a
WWE professional wrestler.

The WWF noticed Lesnar's wrestling success. In 2000, the organization's leaders asked him to join the WWF. Lesnar signed a contract with the WWF and was sent to train in the Ohio Valley Wrestling program that year. There, he trained with future wrestling stars John Cena, Randy Orton, and Dave Batista.

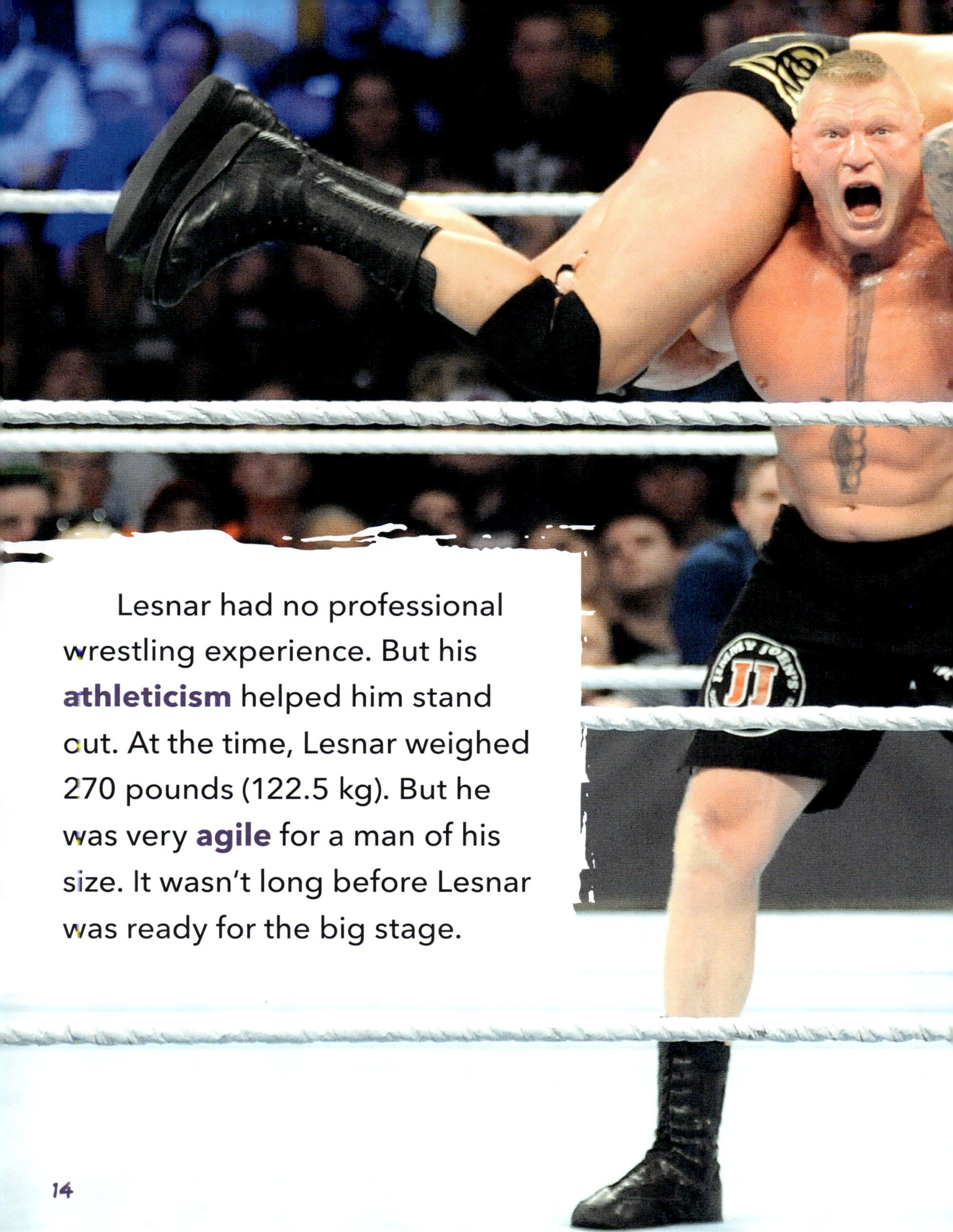

Lesnar had no professional wrestling experience. But his **athleticism** helped him stand out. At the time, Lesnar weighed 270 pounds (122.5 kg). But he was very **agile** for a man of his size. It wasn't long before Lesnar was ready for the big stage.

In 2016, Lesnar defeated Orton at SummerSlam.

CHAPTER 4

A HUGE FIRST IMPRESSION

Lesnar made his WWF **debut** at Monday Night Raw in March 2002. There, he earned his nickname "the Next Big Thing." The main event match featured Allen "Al Snow" Sarven, Maven Huffman, and Matthew "Spike Dudley" Hyson.

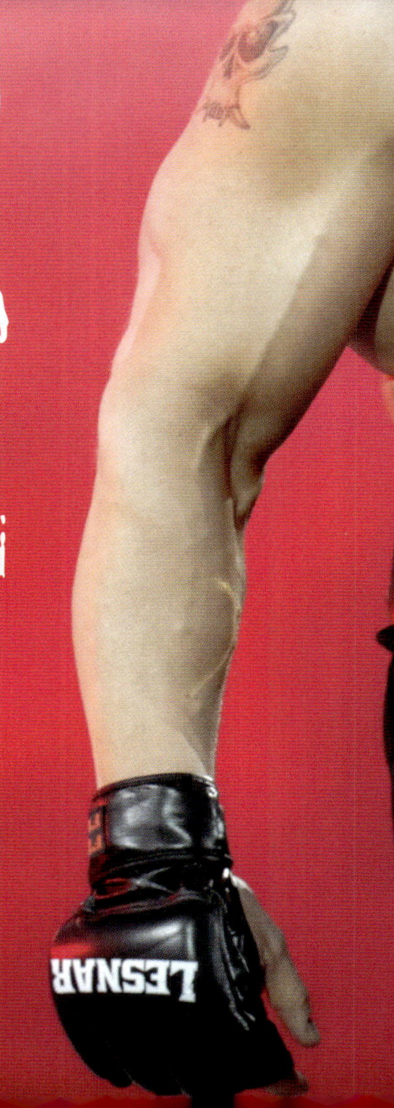

Lesnar with his manager, Paul Heyman. Heyman has been Lesnar's manager ever since his debut. The two are also very good friends outside the ring.

W
JIMMY JO

Once the match began, Lesnar waited outside the ring before joining the fight. He smashed Snow onto a garbage can prop. He then picked up and threw Maven onto the mat. Next, he slammed Dudley onto the mat multiple times. Pro wrestling manager Paul Heyman jumped into the ring, raising Lesnar's arm in victory. The surprised crowd cheered the unknown winner.

XTREME FACT

Lesnar is a "Paul Heyman Guy." That means he is managed by Heyman. Heyman also manages champions Joseph "Roman Reigns" Anoa'i and Kurt Angle.

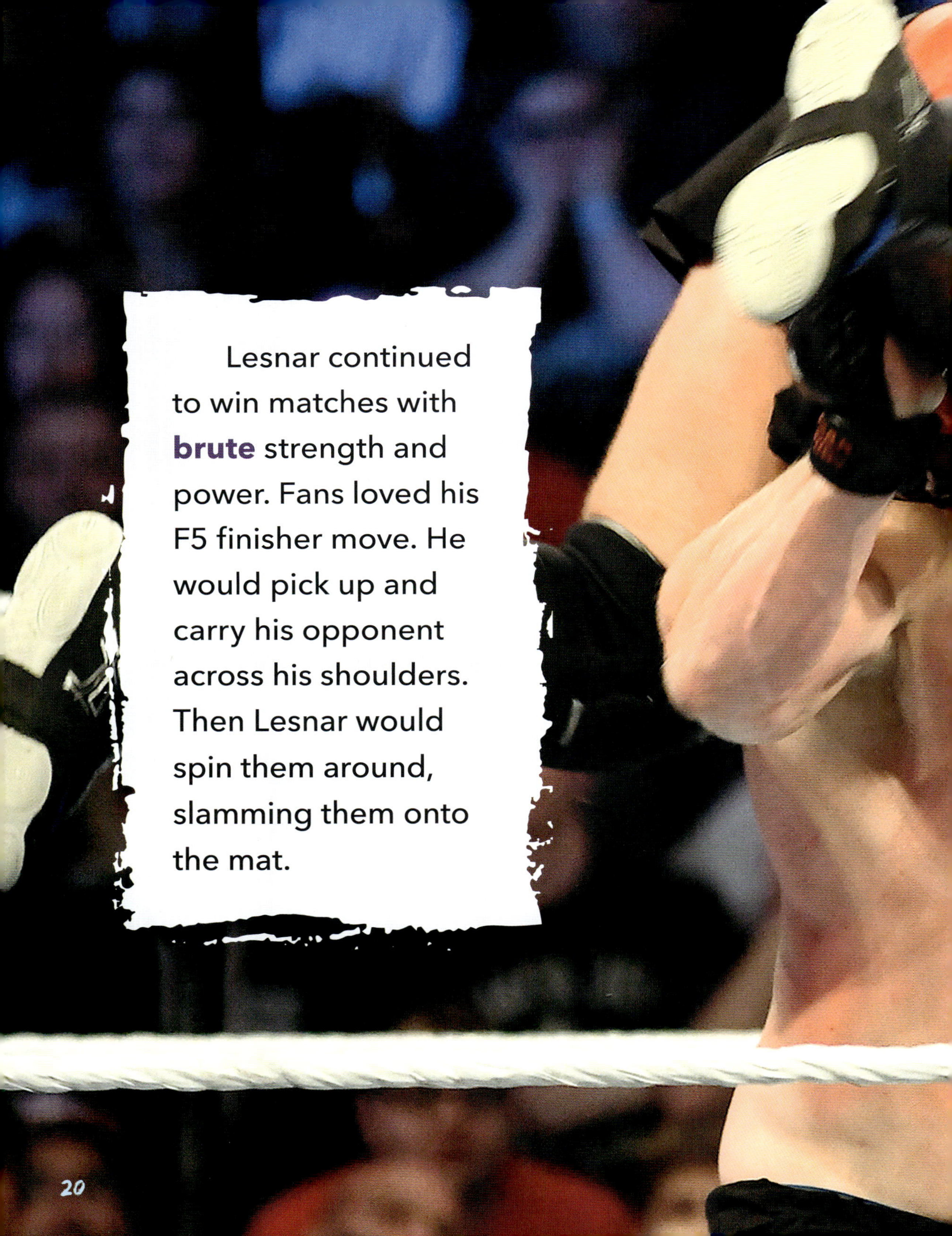

Lesnar continued to win matches with **brute** strength and power. Fans loved his F5 finisher move. He would pick up and carry his opponent across his shoulders. Then Lesnar would spin them around, slamming them onto the mat.

Lesnar using his F5 move on Nuufolau "Samoa Joe" Seanoa during a Fatal 4 Way match in 2017

CHAPTER 5

A RAPID RISE

Lesnar **overpowered** almost all of his opponents. In June 2002, Lesnar fought in the King of the Ring **tournament**. He defeated all the other wrestlers and earned a shot at winning the WWE championship title during SummerSlam in August 2002.

Nassau Coliseum

Lesnar fights Dwayne "the Rock" Johnson at SummerSlam in the Nassau Coliseum in New York.

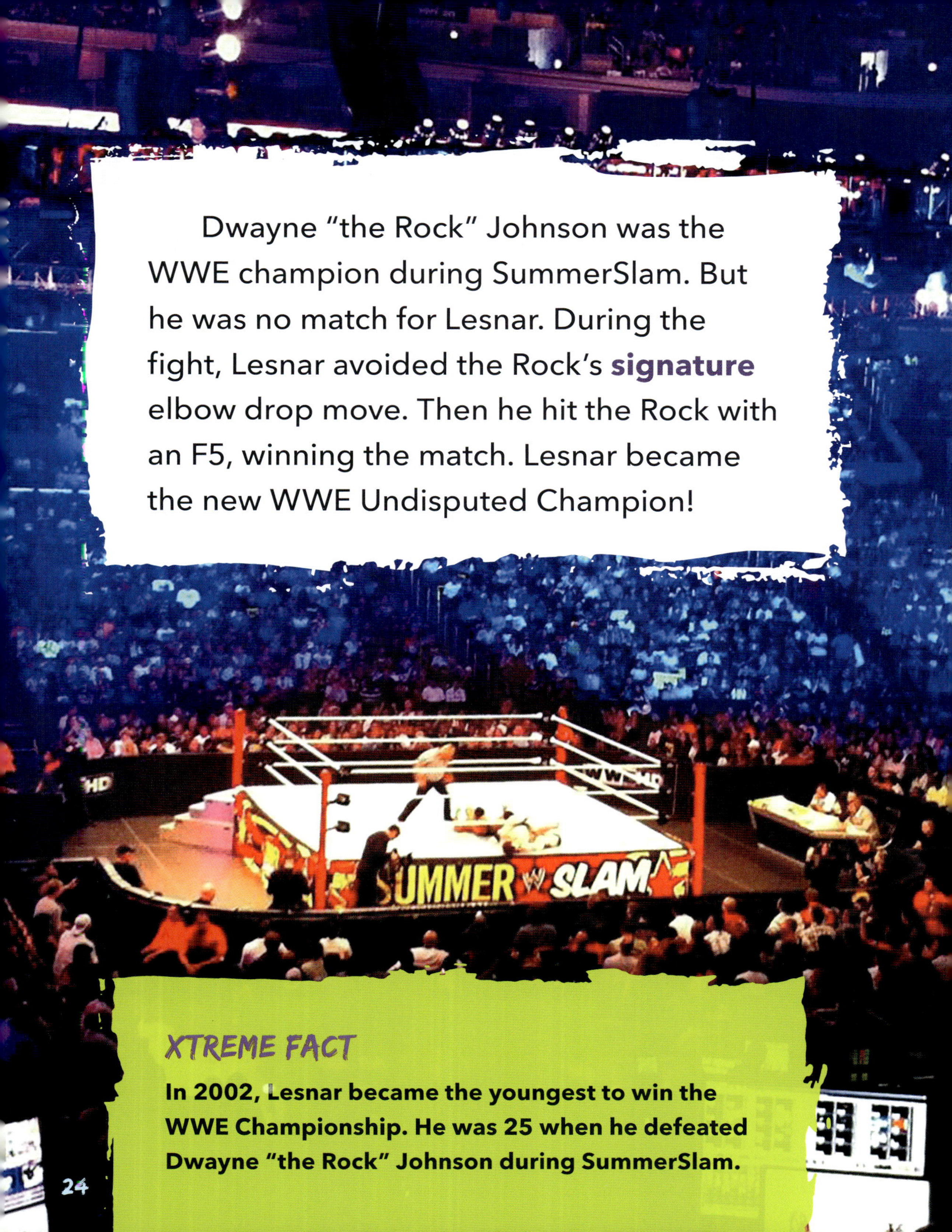

Dwayne "the Rock" Johnson was the WWE champion during SummerSlam. But he was no match for Lesnar. During the fight, Lesnar avoided the Rock's **signature** elbow drop move. Then he hit the Rock with an F5, winning the match. Lesnar became the new WWE Undisputed Champion!

XTREME FACT

In 2002, Lesnar became the youngest to win the WWE Championship. He was 25 when he defeated Dwayne "the Rock" Johnson during SummerSlam.

Lesnar raising the championship belt in victory after defeating the Rock during the 2016 SummerSlam

CHAPTER 6

CHAMPIONSHIP FIGHTS

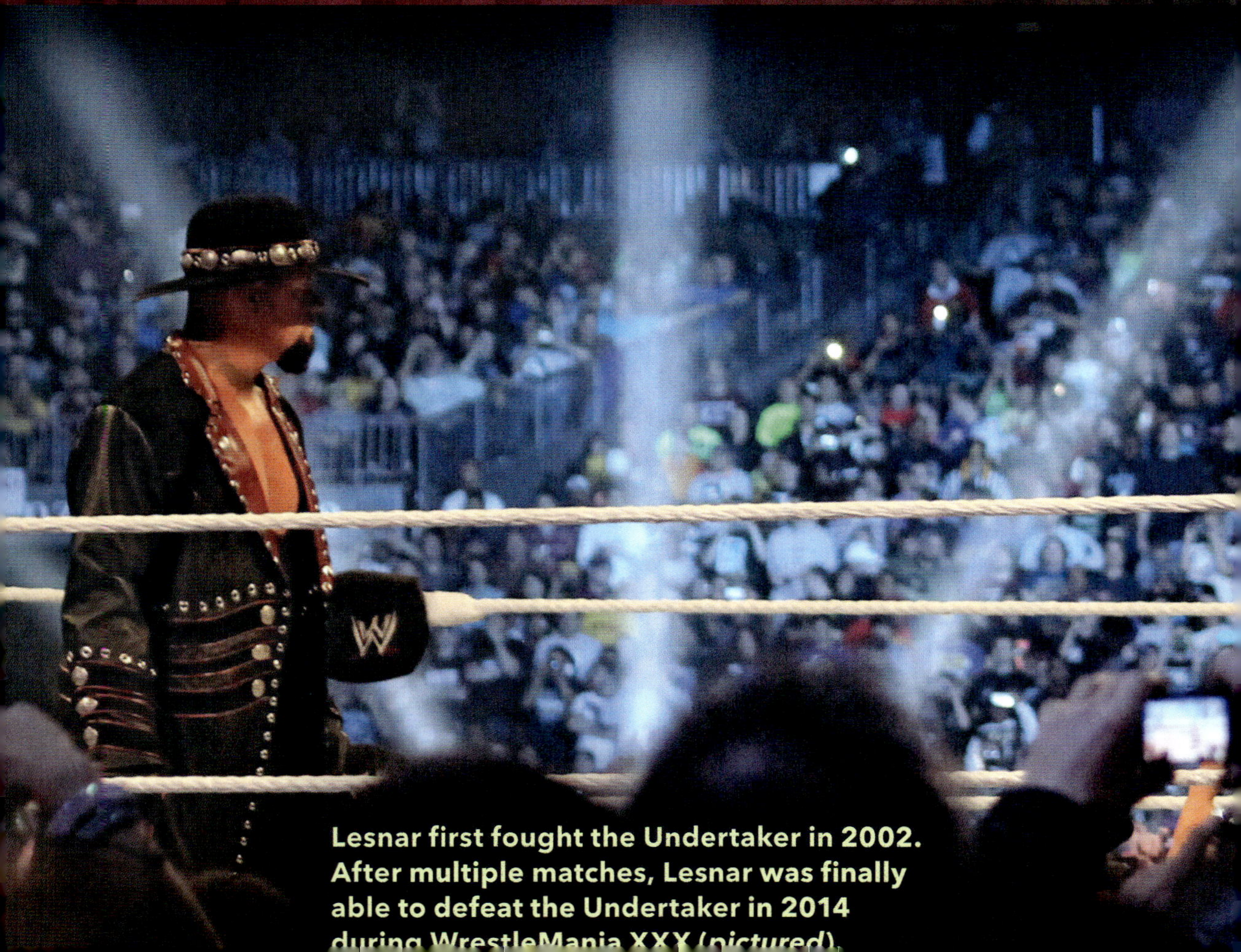

Lesnar first fought the Undertaker in 2002. After multiple matches, Lesnar was finally able to defeat the Undertaker in 2014 during WrestleMania XXX (*pictured*).

Later that year, Lesnar successfully **defended** the championship against the Undertaker and Adam "Edge" Copeland. He lost the title belt to Paul "the Big Show" Wight in November during the 2002 Survivor Series. It was the first time Lesnar was successfully pinned at a WWE event. In the following months, Lesnar would fight to win back the championship.

Lesnar defeated Kurt Angle (*right*) in 2003, winning his third WWE Championship.

In March 2003, Lesnar beat Kurt Angle during SmackDown, winning the WWE Championship again. In June, Lesnar faced the Big Show. Lesnar lifted the 500-pound (226.8 kg) wrestler. He slammed the Big Show onto the mat, breaking the ring!

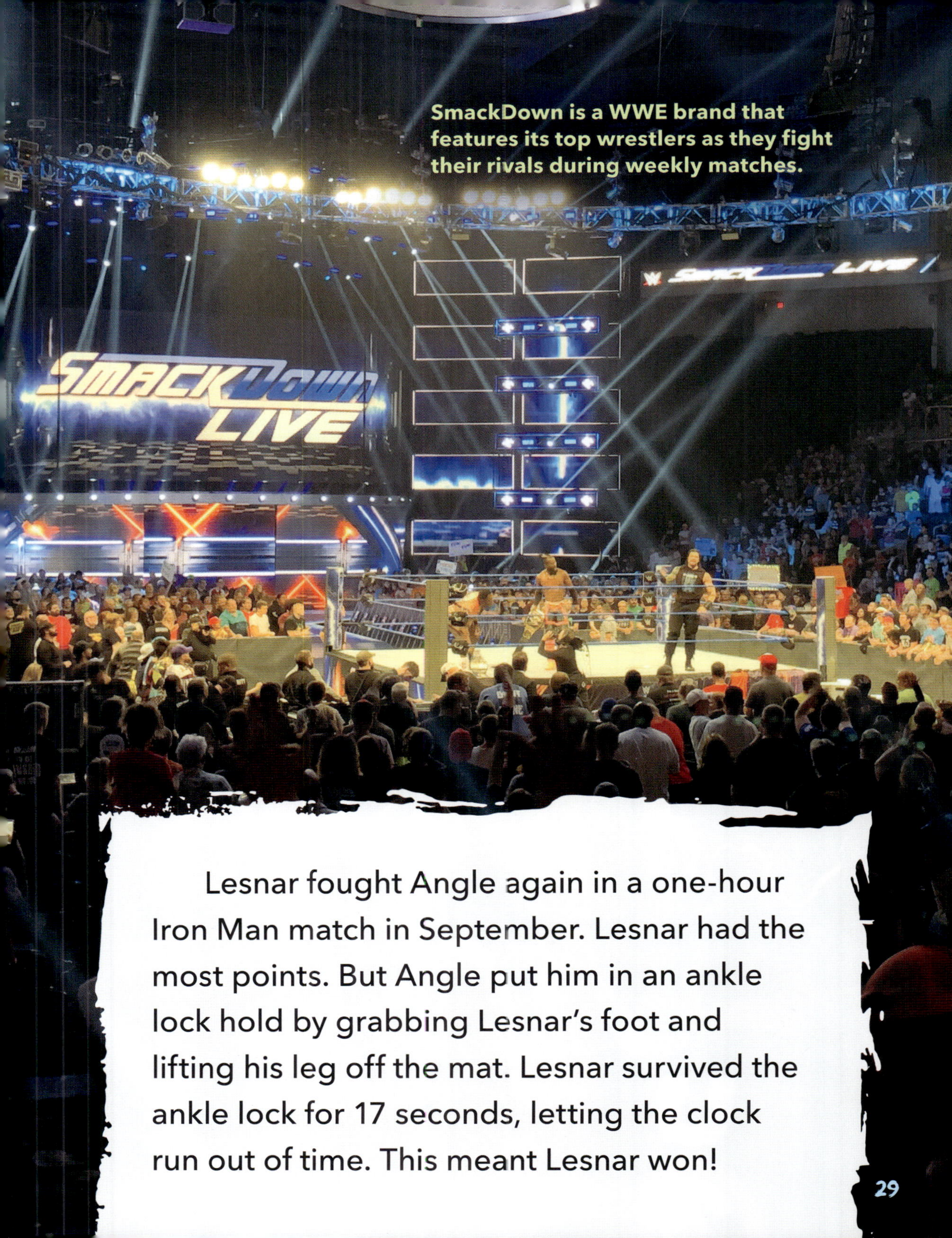

Lesnar fought Angle again in a one-hour Iron Man match in September. Lesnar had the most points. But Angle put him in an ankle lock hold by grabbing Lesnar's foot and lifting his leg off the mat. Lesnar survived the ankle lock for 17 seconds, letting the clock run out of time. This meant Lesnar won!

CHAPTER 7

TRYING DIFFERENT SPORTS

In 2004, Lesnar wanted a new challenge. He took a break from wrestling to play professional football. Lesnar tried out for the Minnesota Vikings, a National Football League team. Unfortunately, Lesnar did not make the team.

Lesnar (*right*) trains with Chris Hovan (*left*), during a Minnesota Vikings football training camp.

Lesnar returned to MMA in 2016 to compete at UFC 200. He fought Mark Hunt (*bottom*) and won!

XTREME FACT

Lesnar won four out of seven fights when he competed in the UFC.

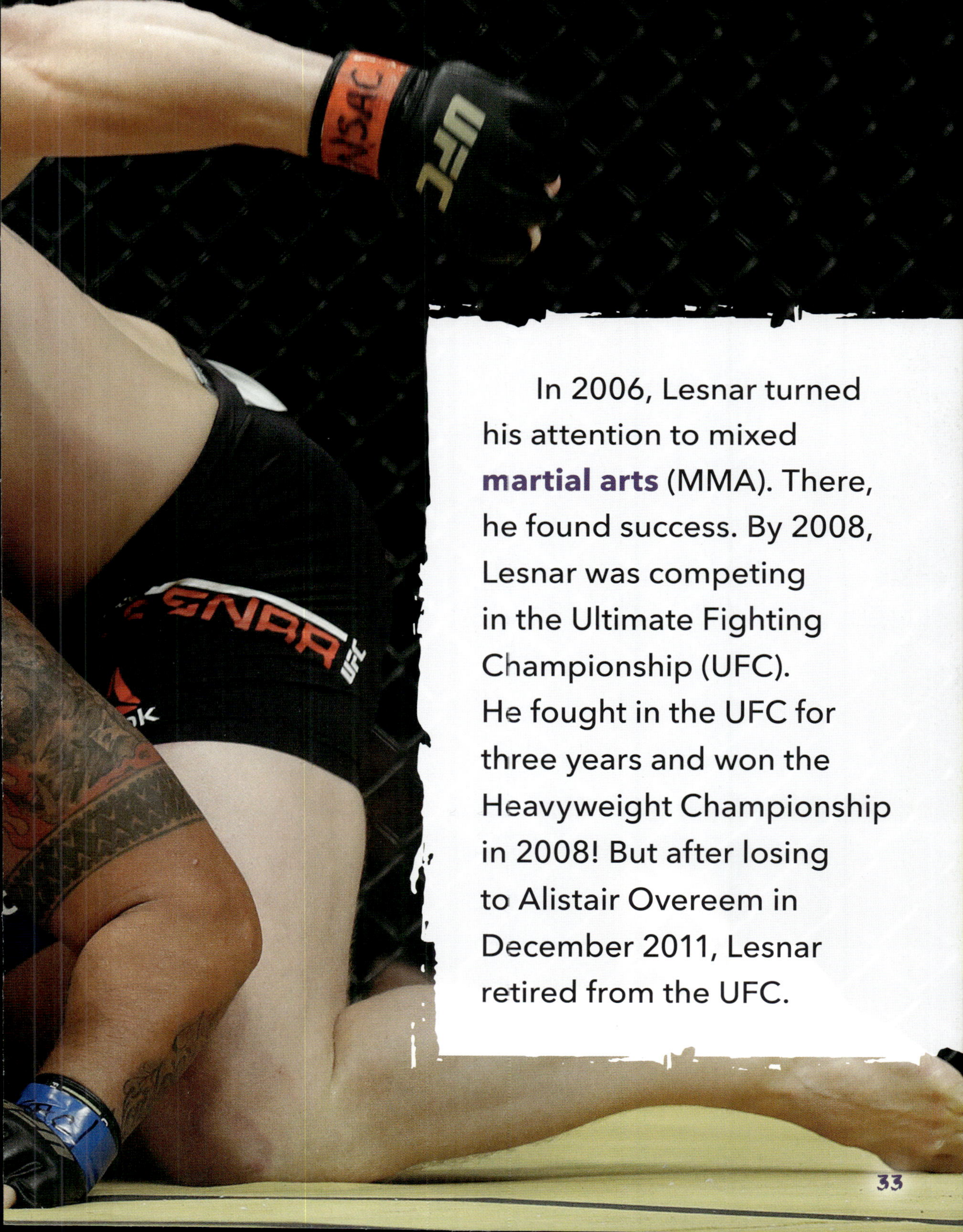

In 2006, Lesnar turned his attention to mixed **martial arts** (MMA). There, he found success. By 2008, Lesnar was competing in the Ultimate Fighting Championship (UFC). He fought in the UFC for three years and won the Heavyweight Championship in 2008! But after losing to Alistair Overeem in December 2011, Lesnar retired from the UFC.

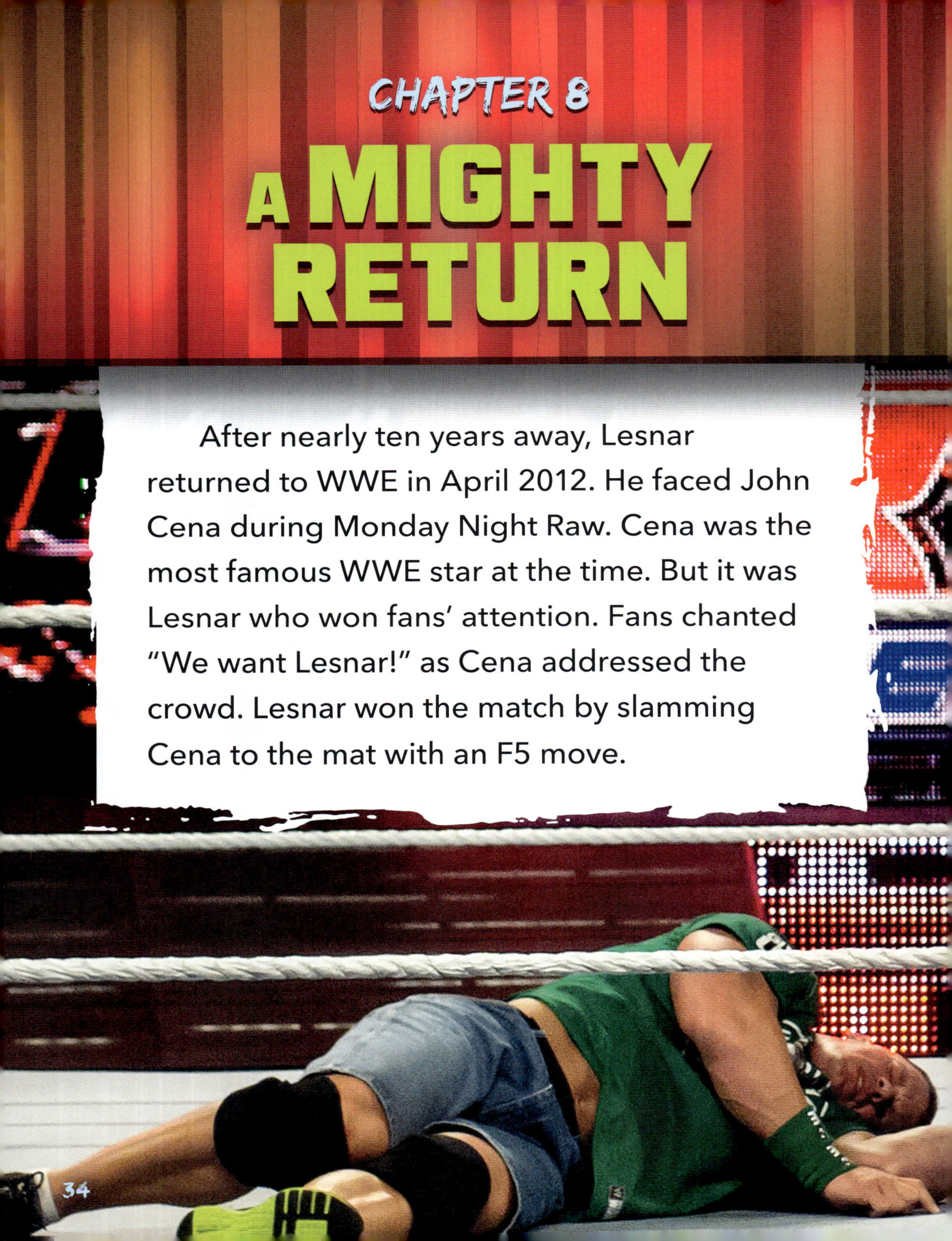

CHAPTER 8

A MIGHTY RETURN

After nearly ten years away, Lesnar returned to WWE in April 2012. He faced John Cena during Monday Night Raw. Cena was the most famous WWE star at the time. But it was Lesnar who won fans' attention. Fans chanted "We want Lesnar!" as Cena addressed the crowd. Lesnar won the match by slamming Cena to the mat with an F5 move.

Lesnar stands over John Cena after defeating him during Monday Night Raw.

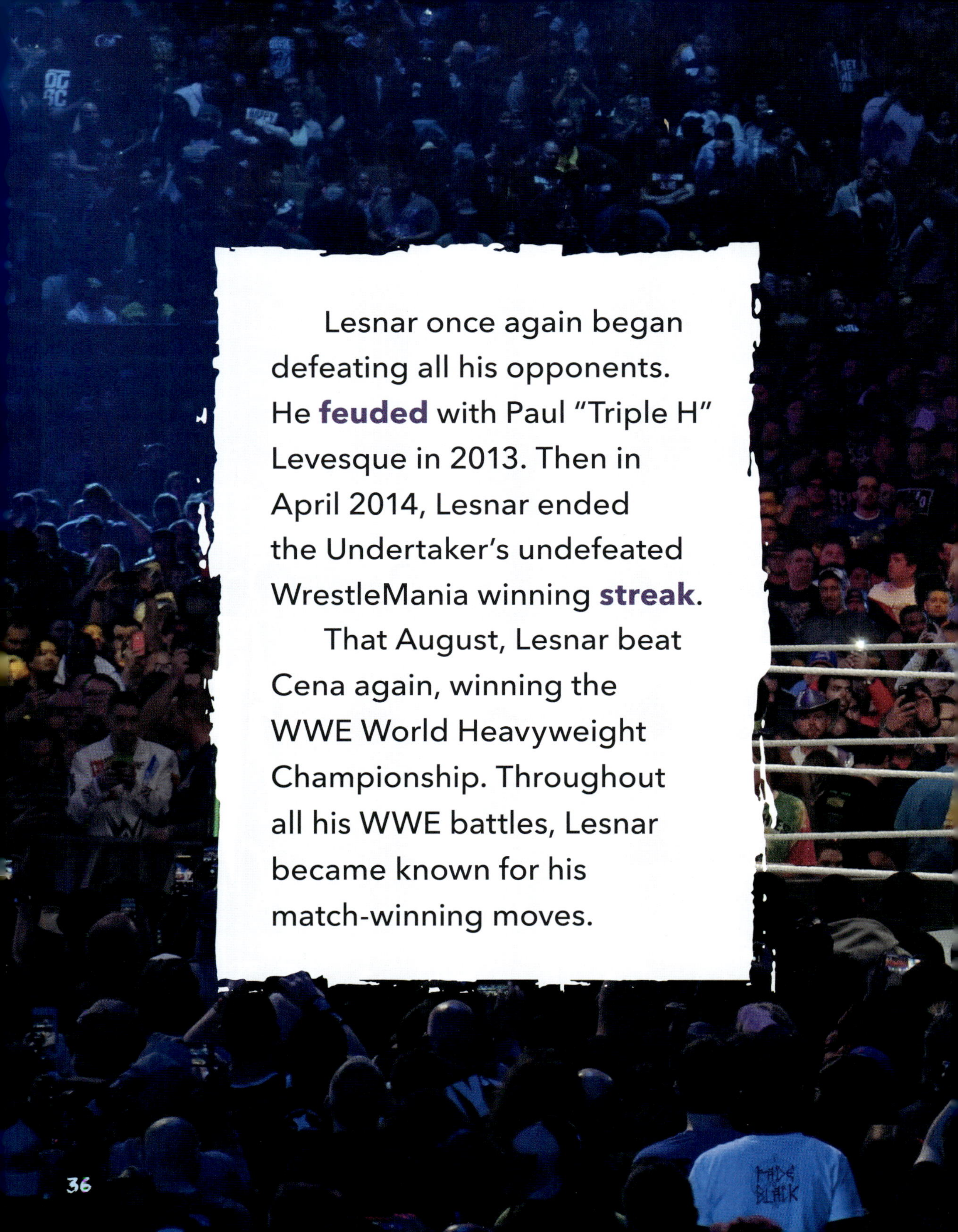

Lesnar once again began defeating all his opponents. He **feuded** with Paul "Triple H" Levesque in 2013. Then in April 2014, Lesnar ended the Undertaker's undefeated WrestleMania winning **streak**.

That August, Lesnar beat Cena again, winning the WWE World Heavyweight Championship. Throughout all his WWE battles, Lesnar became known for his match-winning moves.

In 2018, Lesnar defeated Joseph "Roman Reigns" Anoa'i (*right*) during WrestleMania XXXIV.

CHAPTER 9

FAMOUS MOVES

Lesnar finished many matches with his F5 move. He was also famous for his suplex move. He would grab an opponent's waist from behind. Then, he would lift them over his head and slam them backward onto the mat.

Lesnar **overpowered** many opponents with these moves. But one rival proved challenging.

XTREME FACT

After his WWE return, Lesnar wasn't a full-time wrestler. So, he didn't have to compete hundreds of times a year. This allowed his muscles to recover between matches.

CHAPTER 10

GETTING GOLDBERG

One wrestler Lesnar was unable to defeat was William Goldberg. The two fought in 2004 and 2016. Lesnar lost both times. In 2017, they met again. But this time was different.

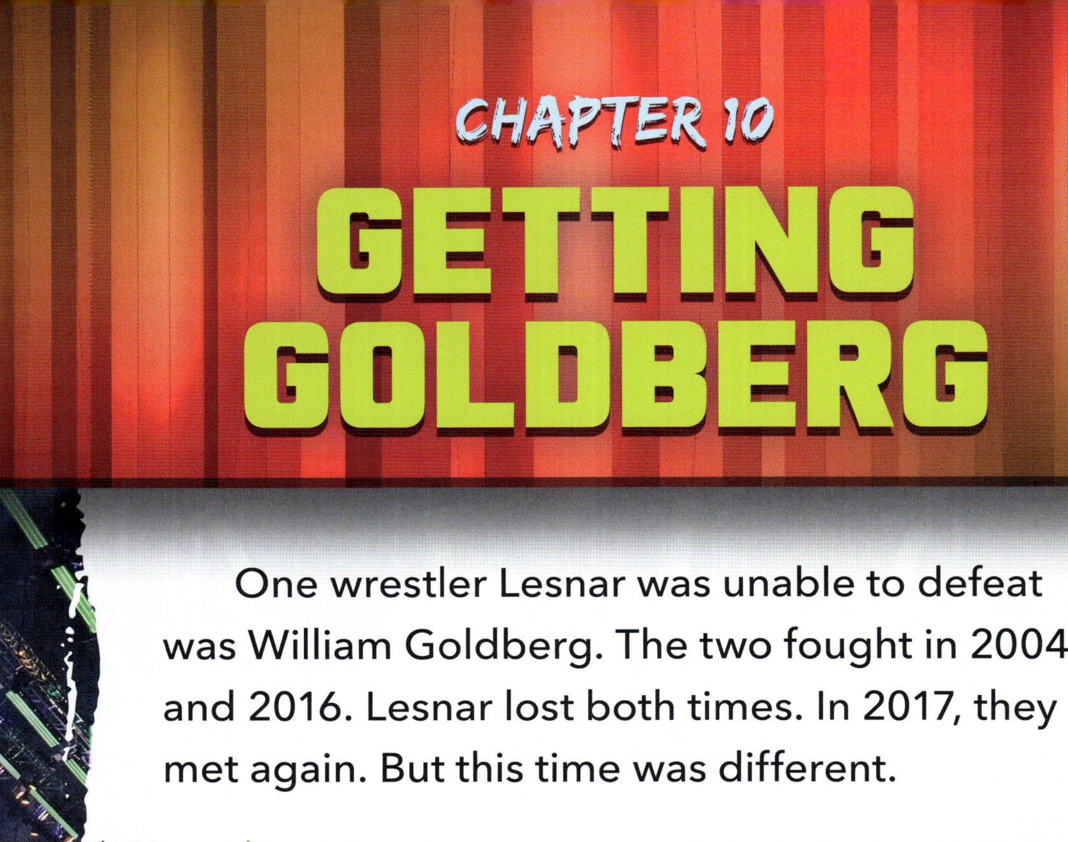

WrestleMania XXXIII

Lesnar and Goldberg fought at WrestleMania XXXIII for the Universal Championship. Goldberg smashed Lesnar with prop spears. But Lesnar used ten suplex moves before pinning Goldberg, winning the Universal Championship!

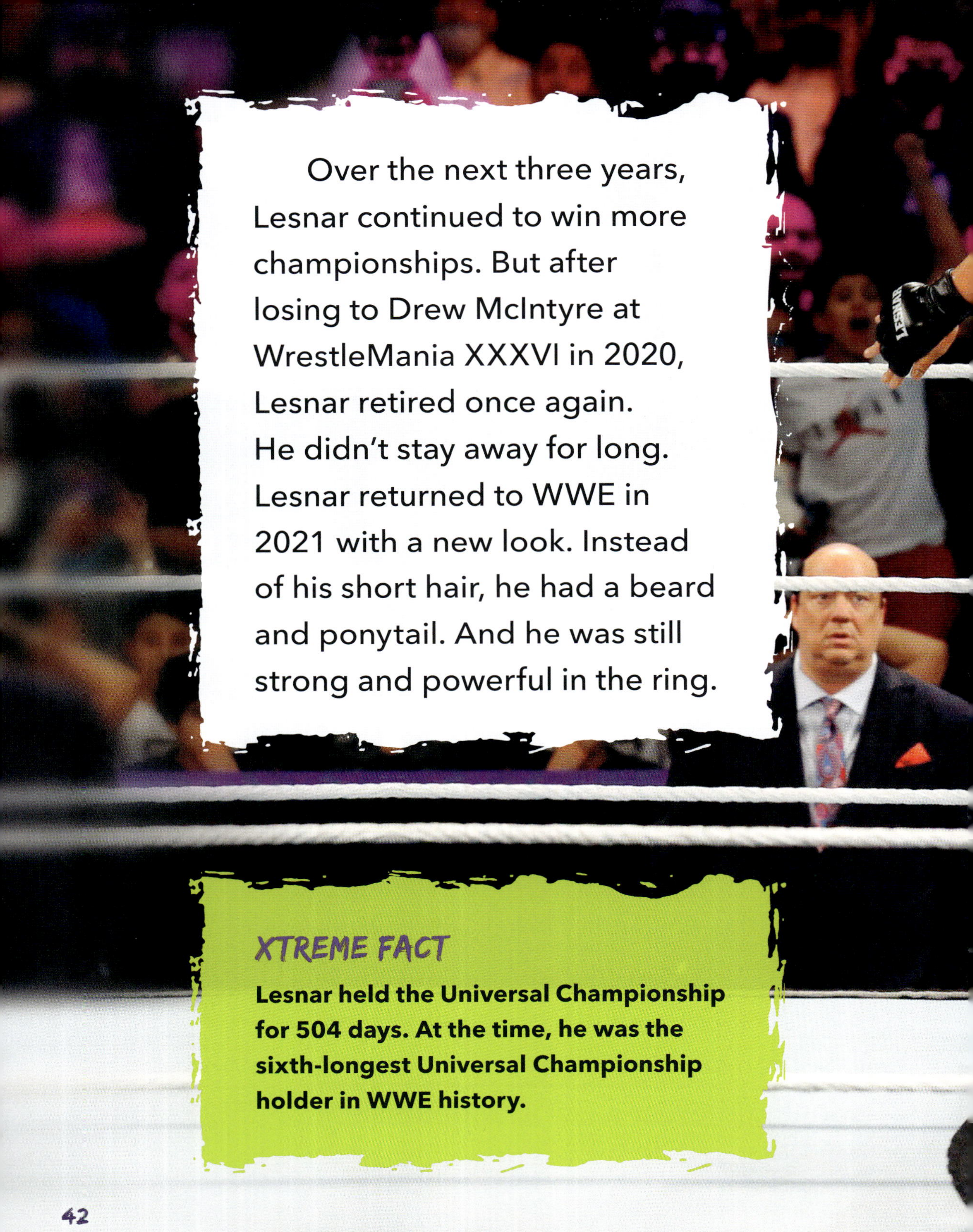

Over the next three years, Lesnar continued to win more championships. But after losing to Drew McIntyre at WrestleMania XXXVI in 2020, Lesnar retired once again. He didn't stay away for long. Lesnar returned to WWE in 2021 with a new look. Instead of his short hair, he had a beard and ponytail. And he was still strong and powerful in the ring.

XTREME FACT

Lesnar held the Universal Championship for 504 days. At the time, he was the sixth-longest Universal Championship holder in WWE history.

Lesnar fights Reigns during the 2021 WWE Crown Jewel event.

A FORCE OF NATURE

Growing up, Lesnar never dreamed he would be one of WWE's biggest stars. But that's exactly what he became. Fans considered him to be wrestling royalty. From his time in WWE to his MMA career, Lesnar was hard to beat. He remained a big **competitor** and top entertainer for decades!

XTREME CHALLENGE

TAKE THE QUIZ BELOW AND PUT WHAT YOU'VE LEARNED TO THE TEST!

1) What wrestling program did Brock Lesnar wrestle with before joining the WWF?

2) What sport did Lesnar try out for after he left WWE for the first time?

3) When you grow up, do you want to travel a lot for your job?

4) Whose undefeated WrestleMania streak did Lesnar famously end in 2014?

5) What would be the benefits of not owning a TV?

GLOSSARY

agile—able to move quickly and easily.

amazing—causing wonder or surprise.

athleticism—the qualities that are characteristic of an athlete, or a person who is trained or skilled in sports.

brute—purely physical.

competitor—one who competes in a sport, contest, or game.

debut—a first appearance.

defend—to protect from harm or attack.

equipment—a set of tools or items used for a special purpose or activity.

feud—to have a long-lasting fight or disagreement.

martial arts—any of several arts of combat and self-defense that are practiced as a sport.

overpower—to overcome by greater force.

recruit—to increase the number of a group or organization by enlisting new members.

signature—something such as a tune, style, or logo that serves to set apart or identify.

streak—a consecutive series.

stunt—an unusual or daring action used to gain attention.

tournament—a series of contests or games played to win a championship.

ONLINE RESOURCES

To learn more about Brock Lesnar, please visit **abdobooklinks.com** or scan this QR code. These links are routinely monitored and updated to provide the most current information available.

INDEX